IN THE COMPANY OF MONSTERS

23 September 2023 – 24 February 2024

IN THE COMPANY OF MONSTERS
NEW VISIONS, ANCIENT MYTHS

Edited by Emma Aston and Andrew Mangham

Published for the exhibition held from 23 September 2023 – 27 January 2024 at Reading Museum, Blagrave Street, Reading, RG1 1QH.

© University of Reading, 2023.

ISBN: 978-0-70491587-9

All rights reserved. No part of this publication may be transmitted in any form or by any means, electronic or mechanical, including photocopy, recording, or any storage and retrieval system, without prior written permission.

Catalogue edited by Emma Aston and Andrew Mangham.

Catalogue designed and typeset by Richard André and Apinaya Ganeshalingam, students in the Department of Typography & Graphic Communication, University of Reading.

Front cover designed by Richard André and Apinaya Ganeshalingam.

Cover image: Paul Reid, Cyclops (2014). © Paul Reid. Courtesy of 108 Fine Art.

Printed and bound by Gomer Press.

Contents

7   Acknowledgements

8   Artists' biographies

10 The Monstrosity of Anatomy: The Artwork of Eleanor Crook
    Kelley Swain

14 Return to Arcadia: Pathos and Poetry in the Paintings of Paul Reid
    Bill Hare

19 Worshipping Monsters
    Emma Aston

22 Heracles, Sea Monsters and Other Snaky Characters: A Story of Good versus Evil?
    Amy Smith

26 Classical Monsters Today
    Dunstan Lowe

30 Nature's Experiments: Monsters in Science and Literature
    Andrew Mangham

34 Catalogue

Acknowledgements

Putting together this exhibition has involved many people and organizations, all of whom deserve our deepest gratitude. Our first thanks are due to the artists Eleanor Crook and Paul Reid for kindly agreeing to provide their works and permissions both for the exhibition and the catalogue. We thank them for their patience, generosity, and good spirit on the many occasions we pestered them for information and permissions. We hope the result does justice to their wonderful work. To Elaine Blake at Reading Museum, we owe thanks for believing in this project and in working with us to put it all together. We would like to thank Guja Bandini, Lucy Griffin and Neil Cocks for helping us bring our ideas to a younger audience. Richard André and Apinaya Ganeshalingam from the Department of Typography and Graphic Communication did the beautiful design work on this catalogue; we are grateful to James Lloyd for connecting us with Richard and Apinaya through the Real Jobs scheme and to Rob Banham for his guidance.

This exhibition could not have taken place without support from the Interdisciplinary Research Fund at the University of Reading. We are grateful to the Centre for Health Humanities at Reading for organising this support and to Roberta Gilchrist for her words of advice and encouragement. We are grateful to Marie Randall, Beth Steiner, Charlotte Johnson, David Brauner, Nicola Wilson, and John Gibbs for their help with the research aspects of the project. Thanks to Rachael Scott for her help with registering this catalogue. Naomi Lebens offered some helpful early advice and Rhianedd Smith was a mine of helpful suggestions.

We are grateful to owners of private collections who loaned us their items and to Gemma Batchelor and Theo Albano at the Fleming Collection, India Stewart at 108 Fine Art Gallery, and Fiona Shapcott for assistance with the loans of specific artworks. Thanks to Clare Plascow, Claire Clough, Victoria Stevens, and Fiona Melhuish for helping us select and photograph additional items from the University of Reading's collections, and to Amy Smith and Jayne Holly for agreeing to the migration of some of the Ure Museum's precious ancient monsters down to Reading Museum for the exhibition. Thank also to our undergraduate partners Shona Carter-Griffiths and Megan Davies who worked incredibly hard on helping us put this exhibition together and Tom McCann and the UROP scheme who helped us fund their time. We are grateful to all of our student volunteers. We are grateful to the Hellenic Society and the University of Reading Arts Committee for their support and to the University of Reading's Marketing, Communication and Engagement team for their help. Finally, we would like to thank Bill Hare, Dunstan Lowe, Amy Smith, and Kelley Swain for their contributions to this catalogue, plus Justine Hopkins, Louise Johnson, Jordan Miller, and Jaroslav Svelch for contributing to our public lecture series.

Artists' biographies

Eleanor Crook is a British sculptor with a special interest in mortality, anatomy and pathology, who exhibits internationally in fine art and medical and science museum contexts. She studied Classics and Philosophy at Oxford before training in sculpture at Central St Martins and the Royal Academy Schools in the early 90s, where she specialised in wax modeling, lost wax bronze casting and other lifelike media. She pieced together a knowledge of Anatomy from London's medical museums and the dissection room as a medical artist, finding figurative art to be not in favour at the time; even so, her Classical background meant that communing with statues, and therefore the body, were second nature. Crook considers her work 'more effigy than statue', as they are imbued with a convincing sense of life.

She has developed close, long-term collaborations with medical museums and historic anatomical wax collections such as the Gordon Museum of Pathology, Guy's Hospital, Ghent University Museum, and the Vrolik Museum Amsterdam, where she continues wax modeling traditions and combines research through human dissection and studying the history of anatomical model-making. Most recently, she has worked with museum project partners on creating a genre of anatomical Expressionism, uncanny yet rooted in medical investigation, mythology, and the mysteries of the mind.

To learn more about Eleanor Crook, her work, and find selected art for sale, visit www.eleanorcrook.net.

Paul Reid was born in Scone, Perth, in 1975. Between 1994 and 1998, he studied at Duncan of Jordanstone College of Art, Dundee, where he obtained First Class honours in drawing and painting. Since then his work has been part of a number of major exhibitions, in Scotland and northern England in particular, but also in Europe. He has accompanied the then Prince of Wales on visits to Italy, Turkey, Jordan and Canada, drawing and painting the landscapes and people encountered. He is firmly established as an artist who combines technical mastery with striking new visions of ancient myths.

On the face of it, Reid's work is traditional in medium (oil; charcoal), though he has more recently moved into the use of digital technology. Within the traditional aesthetic, however, lies a world of the unexpected: uncanny hybrids of human and animal; juxtapositions of ancient myths with modern landscapes, faces, buildings. Central to every work is storytelling: characters from Greek mythology are caught at tense moments in their narrative, at some point of shocked discovery or on the very edge of violence; or else they pause in strange stillness, allowed a moment's repose even as the next (perhaps final) act of the mythical drama impends. The seated Minotaur is a perfect example: he sits easily, casually, but the ancient story dictates what is shortly to befall him. To work with ancient myths is to work with stories that have been told and retold for millennia. This is not to say that they cannot be reshaped; they always have been. Reid's reshapings are subtle, but they leave the viewer in no doubt that ancient men, women, monsters and gods have a place in the modern world as they did in the distant world that first created them.

To learn more about Paul Reid and his work, and find selected art for sale, visit www.paulreidart.co.uk.

Eustache 'Jerk' Dupree, the Icarus Man of Pontchartoula, by Eleanor Crook

Kelley Swain

Kelley Swain is a writer specialising in subjects from the history of science and medicine. She writes extensively as an art and culture critic for *The Lancet* medical journals, and is the author of numerous works of poetry, fiction, and non-fiction. She lives in Australia's far-flung island state, where she is currently a PhD candidate in Arts & Health at the University of Tasmania.

The monstrosity of anatomy: The artwork of Eleanor Crook

'Non hic Centauros, non Gorgonas, Harpyasque / Invenies, hominem pagina nostra sapit'.

'*No Centaurs here, or Gorgons look to find, / My subject is of man and humankind*', writes Robert Burton in his famous tome, *The Anatomy of Melancholy*, which runs to over 1,000 pages in its efforts to 'anatomize' (or dissect) the very nature of man. In mentioning Centaurs and Gorgons, Burton means that these Classical monsters are often used to represent extremes of the human, for good or ill.

I had an opportunity to sit with Eleanor Crook in her garden workshop on a May evening in 2017, rain ticking musically on the wooden roof. Beside us, unavoidably centre-stage, lay a two-metre-long block of lime-wood, from which a morbidly cadaverous, incomplete body was beginning to appear. Crook was carving the first Transi, or cadaver tomb, to be made in over 400 years. Transi means 'I have passed over' in Latin. Even in its early stages, this Transi, lovingly named 'Guy the Gaunt', was already showing Crook's signature style, blending anatomical accuracy with haunting morbidity – and a little wink.

Eleanor Crook is arguably the most skilled living sculptor of anatomical, medical, and pathological art. An array of fascinating, grotesque, and provocative projects made by Crook can be found on show in galleries and museums across the UK and Europe. Her work claims gorgons, harpies and hybrids; it claims centaur-beasts in her half-Nietzsche, half-cow sculpture *Nietzsche-Cow/Dionysus*, and in her half-man, half-fried-chicken sculpture, *Eustace 'Jerk' Dupree, the Icarus Man of Ponchatoula*. Crook's work admits that the subject – of man and humankind – is, emotionally and metaphorically, the Centaur or Gorgon, the transcendence or the horror.

Many of Crook's artworks are hybrids, chimeras, and monsters referencing Classical antiquity. This is a branch of Crook's work where playfulness is allowed free rein, though anatomical accuracy is ever-present. Here, we meet hybrids and chimeras in wax, wood, and bronze, and see the influence of Crook's first degree in Classics and Philosophy at Magdalen College, Oxford. Crook considered a career in Classics after Oxford, but was drawn to making her own art. The influence of mythology on her work never left, and the style she has come to call 'Anatomical Expressionism' revealed itself early, during her art foundation year in 1989. When I interviewed Crook in 2019 for *The Lancet* medical journal (vol. 394, p. 293), she explained that she discovered her peers' 'interruptions' to the sculptural or painterly surface of the head made their work look like modern art. But on her work, she explained, it looked like injury, or a disease. This inevitable tendency led her into medical and pathological art.

Crook has made a name crafting her uncanny sculptures, as well as teaching on the Forensic Anthropology course at the University of Dundee, leading summer schools in anatomy and facial reconstruction at the Ruskin School of Art at the University of Oxford, running regular workshops in medical moulage, and accepting commissions for unique pieces, including the magnificent *Santa Medicina* for the Medicine Galleries in London's Science Museum, the gut-churning *Consolation of Pharmacology* for the Royal Pharmaceutical Society, and that uncanny Transi for the University of Winchester, *Guy the Gaunt*.

When COVID-19 lockdowns landed Crook at home, more recently, she took the opportunity to explore print-making and painting in ways she had not had time to practise in years. She launched several courses on Morbid Anatomy, drawing on teaching she had done at the Ruskin School of Art, delving into Jungian psychoanalysis and dream theory. This called forth her Classical influences, and created a second Icarus – previously in wax, now in mixed media – in 'Icarus over the Volcanoes', a favourite character of antiquity. To Crook, Icarus represents 'the dangers of ambition, but also the dangers of staying put – but also the exhilaration of danger and the beauty of the journey'.

The words 'monster', 'hybrid', and 'chimera' are as slippery and amorphous as the things they set out to describe. Their most powerful form of shape-shifting exists in the no-man's land wherein they can function as metaphors, literal descriptions, or both at once. What can be solved in being dissolved? As Marina Warner writes, the two-faced role of the monster means both 'I demonstrate' (*monstro*) and 'I warn' (*moneo*).

Monsters are made manifest most readily in art, and especially Crook's work, as she pushes the forms and boundaries of wax, bronze, wood, and paint. Stepping beyond the canvas in recent explorations with image-generating Artificial Intelligence software, Crook considers AI 'a kind of hundred-thousand-headed hybrid, as it pools the history of images into a powerful and amoral collage engine'. She creates beasts, but of the most human kind, and makes us ask: what do these demons demonstrate? As we witness what Stephen T. Asma calls 'desires, cravings, fears, anxieties so powerful as to make us feel alienated from our very selves', myths of heroes grappling with monsters take on new meaning.

If to study the artwork of Eleanor Crook is to investigate the tradition of the morbid, the macabre, and the monstrous; it is also to consider a long line of anatomically-interested artists (and artistically-interested anatomists) from antiquity to the present, from Andreas Vesalius to Francis Bacon: those who did not shy away from stripping back the skin, literally or emotionally, from the human frame. Crook's theory and practice of Anatomical Expressionism argues that 'there is an art movement that began when artists started investigating the insides of the body and continues throughout history, a fraternity of insider knowledge. Those who have clapped eyes on our actual physical components, via dissections, corpses and occasionally live surgery, have learned their anatomy in a vividly unforgettable way'.

If to study Crook's work is to study illness and death, it is also to study the muscular tensegrity of the body (man or beast, or both) in the tradition of Eugène Delacroix and Auguste Rodin. The Centaur or Gorgon, the transcendence or the horror? Sometimes there is a monster in the cave, breathing beside us in the dark – and sometimes the monster in the cave, breathing in the dark, is us.

Minotaur, by Paul Reid

Bill Hare

Bill Hare studied at the Universities of Edinburgh and London. He taught art history at the University of Edinburgh, Edinburgh College of Art and the Open University. He was also Exhibition Organiser at the Talbot Rice Gallery. He is now a free-lance curator and writer on Scottish art since 1945, publishing books and catalogues on that period. He is an Honorary Fellow at the University of Edinburgh.

Return to Arcadia: Pathos and poetry in the paintings of Paul Reid

'Poetry is more serious than history'.

Paul Reid is a rare phenomenon in today's art world; he is an academic history painter. Most of his contemporaries are either unaware of, or uninterested in, this artistic genre; but that was not always the case. In the 18th and 19th centuries, when the art academies were by far the most powerful culture institutions in Europe, artists with high ambitions would invariably aspire to the elevated status of history painter. This required, not only outstanding technical skill in drawing and painting, but also, an in-depth knowledge of the classics from which to draw upon for appropriate subject matter. For the only legitimate source of pictorial subjects for a true history painter was sacred or classical texts. As can be seen Reid continues to follow this convention by searching through ancient myths and the writings of Homer and Ovid for the inspiring subject content of his paintings.

What particularly attracted academic painters and their patrons to history painting was the epic universal themes that their art addressed, and always at their thematic core, was the elemental conflict between good and evil. This eternal struggle was played out between the same basic protagonists- the stalwart hero and his dastardly mutant enemies. On the side of virtue and order stood the hero who, from Hercules onwards, always had to be physically and morally strong and unflinching in his single-minded determination to fulfil his divinely appointed destiny. On the other side, in marked contrast, was his multi-facetted adversaries who could take on many different aggressive and seductive forms- from male or female, to animal or even plant. These monstrous creatures were truly protean beings.

While the pictorial depiction of the hero in history painting remained relatively constant right up to the end of the academic era in the 19th century, his combatant markedly changed from era to era. In Antiquity, monsters, as depicted on vase paintings, were either aberrations of the natural order, or malformed offspring of the gods themselves- such as the cyclops Polyphemus, son of Poseidon. Moving into the Christian era, with its obsession of eternal redemption and condemnation, monsters were conscripted into the role of satanic devils, forever tormenting the Damned in Hell. By contrast, the classically minded artists of the Renaissance were far too much taken up with idealising the heroic male figure to show much interest in portraying his monstrous counterpart.

With the Romantic era however, comes the return of the repressed. Monsters are now back with a vengeance as a reaction to the Enlightenment's triumphalism of human reason; most famously depicted by Goya's *The Sleep of Reason Brings Forth Monsters* (1797-9). The monster has now become a creature of the disturbed imagination responding to an ever increasingly oppressive and materialistic society. This fearful situation is most exemplified at the beginning of the modern age by Kafka's harrowing novella *Metamorphosis* (1915). There, both hero and monster, become as one-equal victims of an inscrutable bureaucratic system. Furthermore, in modern painting the Surrealists, under the influence of Freud's theories of the human mind, set out to release the monstrous from the deep unconscious as a cathartic outcry against the manifold horrors of the 20th century. Nothing in art however, could match the ultra-horrendous actions and deeds of our own adored monsters in their smart military attire, who were determined to reduce culture and civilisation to 'a handful of dust'. Ironically this 'brave new world' of ours has now become infinitely too monstrous for Reid's archaic monsters, who have wisely retreated back to the peace and safety of their original Doric arcadia.

In his history paintings Paul Reid does adhere to most of the conventions of that particular genre, both in form and content. He renders his classical sources with a high degree of mimetic idealism, and a great deal of research, study and painterly skill has clearly gone into the making of his 'grand machines' of pictorial excellence. In one crucial area however, the artist deliberately transgresses. This is in the manner he treats his mythic narratives contrary to the expected conventions of history painting. Back in the era when history painting was highly admired a great deal of theoretical discourse was concerned with the issue of what particular incident painters should select from the chronology of their literary sources. In 18th century England for instance, Lord

Shaftesbury in his *Notion of the Historical Draught or Tablature of the Judgment of Hercules* (1713) proposed the highly influential idea of the 'pregnant moment'. This concept directed history painters to seek out that vital 'moment' in their visual narrative when- the past circumstances, the present drama and the future consequences of the story line- could coalesce and simultaneously reveal their interrelationship within the layered complexities of a unified pictorial meaning.

In striking contrast, Paul Reid's paintings are less concerned with rendering action, and much more focussed on stillness and reflection. The pregnant moments of violent high drama have long past, leaving a poetic mood that is elegiac rather than epic. Set against a Scottish landscape version of Arcadia, Reid's figure- whether human, monstrous or divine- seem to gaze not at the surrounding scenery, but inwardly on their own meditative thoughts and memories of past glories. They, like the history paintings in which they now find themselves, are no longer deemed relevant to the contemporary art scene; nor to our electronic virtual worlds, where monsters, in every conceivable mutant form, can be supplied for mass entertainment at the press of a computer button. Again, illustrating that each age gets the monsters it deserves.

Finally, it is interesting that the word 'monster' comes from the Latin 'monstrum', meaning a warning, an omen. Keeping this in mind, when we look at Paul Reid's fascinating and intriguing Arcadian scenes, we might, like the figures themselves, ponder on what we have lost- and, what we have put in their place.

Ceramic centaur, perhaps Chiron,
from Lefkandi, Euboea
Circa. 900 BCE, drawn by Rosemary Aston
(© Rosemary Aston, 2021)

Emma Aston

Emma Aston is Professor of Classics at the University of Reading. She wrote her doctoral thesis, and subsequent first book, on the animal-hybrid deities of ancient Greece, and has loved historical monsters ever since. She is also interested in ancient attitudes towards non-human animals, and the role of animals – especially horses – in Classical communities. Full details of her research can be found at www.reading.ac.uk/classics/staff/

Worshipping Monsters

We tend to think of monsters in Greek mythology as the eternal Adversary. They define the hero, through contrast: Herakles and Theseus in particular protect human communities from the scourge of monsters in their various forms: huge beasts like the Nemean Lion; extraordinary beings such as the three-headed Cerberus or the centaur Nessus; or humans of monstrous depravity and violence, such as Sinis, who tore him victims apart by tying them to bent pines and letting go.

Greek myth, however, was never simple. As the essay by Amy Smith in this volume shows, the hero/monster combat did not represent a simple dichotomy between good and bad. Moreover, a rarely acknowledged fact which muddies the water further is this: several significant Greek deities were depicted in the hybrid form normally associated with monstrosity and transgression. So this essay will ask: why did the ancient Greeks worship monsters?

First let me introduce two illustrative examples, Cheiron and Pan. Cheiron was a centaur, half-man, half-horse; Pan had the torso and upright carriage of a human, but the legs, feet and horns, and often the face, of a goat. Neither form seems, on the face of it, to promise the dignity and authority of a god. Centaurs were, on the whole, a riotous bunch, most famous as the people you really didn't want turning up at your wedding reception. When the Lapith Peirithous married Hippodamia, his centaur cousins arrived *en masse*, got drunk, smashed up the furniture, killed several of the guests and tried to abduct the bride. They channelled the dangerous energy – violent, sexual – of the horse. And goats were no better; why did the Athenians choose to worship half-goat Pan, and to do so in the very heart of their city? For that is exactly what they did, and moreover held an annual torch-race in his WWvwhonour, as the fifth century BCE historian tells us (6.105.1). Chiron's cult was less widespread, but it was important in its local area: on Mount Pelion, in Thessaly in northern Greece. What was the point of such monstrous gods?

First, like Dionysus, god of intoxication and transformation, hybrid gods allowed communities to 'own' and control the wildness of the natural world. Pan in Athens was worshipped in a cave on the flank of the Acropolis. He would have been out of place in a temple, alongside Athena and Hephaestus. The cave was his natural habitat, for he was the god of flocks and their herdsmen, of the profusion and danger of the animal and vegetal world. By honouring him within their city, the Athenians brought the outside in, creating a capsule of wild Arcadia (Pan's Peloponnesian homeland) in the midst of civic order. (For Arcadia as a symbolic space for monstrous beings in visual art, see Bill Hare's essay in this volume.) They were also, Herodotus tells us, thanking him for his unexpected help against the Persians at the battle of Marathon in 490 BCE, when his wildness came in useful: he created a sudden panic (the word derives from his name) which routed the Persian foes. His troubling hybrid form, his animal element, made him a being to be courted, not rejected.

What of Chiron? For the Greeks, he was not just different from the other centaurs, famed for his *sophrosyne*, moderation); he was, in effect, an antidote to the savagery they represented. On one memorable occasion he saved the hero Peleus when the other centaurs attacked him. He educated Peleus' son Achilles, as well as a host of other young heroes in the making, teaching them the skills of hunting and healing. It was as a healer that he was worshipped in his sacred cave – another sacred cave – on Pelion. Every year, young men made a pilgrimage up the mountain from the nearby town of Demetrias, dressed in raw fleeces (made temporarily wild, stepping outside the ordered world of their home), to do him honour. Moreover, a local family of healers considered him their ancestor and professional model: they called themselves the Chironidae (descendants of Chiron), specialised in medicinal herbology, and never charged a fee for their services. Their healing plants were harvested on Mount Pelion: thus the fruits of the wild space, like Chiron himself, were drafted into the service of mankind.

What does all this teach us about monsters then, and perhaps even monsters now? Let us imagine the scene, as Herodotus describes it, of 'first contact' between Pan and the Athenians – one particular Athenian, the runner Philippides, who was sent from Marathon to Sparta to request Spartan aid against the Persians (a futile errand, as it turned out). Running north from Laconia, Philippides' way took him through the rugged land of Arcadia. We may imagine him weary, disappointed, struggling over the difficult terrain; suddenly he hears his name called. How does Pan sound? Is his voice a goat's or a man's? Herodotus does not say; but in any case we can imagine the lone runner's terror. Who in these wild uplands knows his name? The appearance of Pan before him cannot have brought any reassurance; one imagines the clack of his hooves on the rocks, his bizarre silhouette as Philippides squints fearfully against the sun. but his words are soothing: if only the Athenians will worship him, he says, he will help them. He has much to offer, though they have not so far realised it.

For the Greeks, then, monsters were not always to be expelled, defeated or destroyed. They have power and value: they represent the energy of nature, which humanity ignores at its peril. The Greeks were no environmentalists: for them the natural world was a palette of resources to be exploited and controlled, and their perspective was largely that of subsistence farmers, staving off hunger by whatever means necessary. But we can see in their monstrous gods, their godly monsters, an acknowledgement that nature has its own agency, that it cannot be expected to co-operate unless given something – honour, offerings, a place within the life of the community – in return for all the wealth it supplies. I shall let the reader take from that whatever lessons might seem applicable to our present times.

Recently in Lerna
by Claire Franklin

"You know, these hydras are just like office work — just when you think you've finished, something new pops up…"

Amy Smith

Amy Smith is a Classical Archaeologist, and the Curator of the Ure Museum of Greek Archaeology in the University of Reading's Classics Department. She is a specialist in ancient ceramics, and is currently engaged in a research project on women and festivals in Classical Athens.

Heracles, sea monsters and other snaky characters: A story of good versus evil?

A trip to the 'hall of mirrors' in an old-fashioned fun fair reminds every child (and adult who dares enter) that anything or anyone might change from good to evil, even beautiful to monstrous, depending on the mirror, lens or frame through which we view them. So might beastly monsters be good, kind or even attractive if we saw them in a positive way? Perhaps we should ask Shrek's wife, Fiona? In his labours and other adventures, the demi-god and 'hero' Heracles (Hercules in Latin) defeats endless monsters. Like most Greek heroes, Heracles isn't perfect: he is a womanizer who eats and drinks too much, suffers from excessive pride and jealousy and gets upset or goes mad when he's not the 'best'. In his battles with 'monsters', we are left asking: who do we judge to be good and who do we consider evil? And if Heracles is so monstrous then why do we call him a hero?

Any battle necessarily has a winner and a loser. *Agon*, 'contest', is the Greek root of the words *protagonist* and *antagonist*, the dramatic characters who are the hero and his enemy, respectively. The difference between these two words is simply in their prefixes, *pro* meaning 'for' and *anti* meaning 'against'. In stories of monsters, perhaps unsurprisingly, ancient Greeks cast their heroes as protagonists by endowing them – as their gods – with human identities and images. Despite his youth and lack of experience, therefore, the infant Heracles easily throttles the snakes Hera sent to attack him and Heracles, his twin-brother, in their crib. If not for this super-human feat – infant Heracles grabs the snakes firmly and decisively – we wouldn't know that Heracles was any less human and mortal than his brother. The grown-up Heracles was victorious when he fought alongside the Olympians in the *gigantomachy*, the gods' epic battle against the earth-born giants. In this contest, as in many others, Heracles was aided by his patron Athena, the goddess of wisdom:cunning and intelligence overwhelm brute force and ignorance. Whoever the foe, Heracles is triumphant, especially with Athena at his side.

Heracles' labours, up to twelve fights with monsters, illustrate the story of civilisation: the defeat of the monster for the sake of protecting the community, which even justifies the killing of a monster. The multi-headed Lernaean hydria, a snaky-headed monster, for example, seemed immortal because they kept growing new heads, but Heracles finally cut off all of the heads and therefore disposed of the monster (see Claire Franklin's 'Recently in Lerna' cartoon, c. 2011). Anthropologists think this hydra refers to the many streams of water around Lerna, a town in Greece's Argive Plain, and that Heracles' defeat of this monster was an engineering feat that solved the problem for the local farmers. Similarly Heracles overpowered river gods, like the Alpheius and Cladeus Rivers in Olympia when – with Athena's help and/or perhaps a crowbar – he rerouted them to clean out the stables of the local King Augeas. Images on Greek pots from the Archaic period (7th-6th centuries BCE) show rivers as: bull-headed, symbolising their strength; and snaky, like the Lernaean hydra, indicating their ability to weave about the landscape. By the Classical period, from 480 BCE, however, the Greeks begin to imagine and image river gods with human heads and even bodies, as on the pediments of the Temple of Zeus at Olympia, ca. 470 BCE. This might reflect the fact that they were almost as strong and powerful as Heracles. While he fought and overpowered them, however, Heracles didn't actually kill river gods. If you visit Olympia today you will find the once mighty Alpheius and Cladeusrivers, albeit in the form of trickling streams. It seems that, from the Classical period (from 480 BCE), Greeks related to their gods on a human scale, whereupon they humanised their gods' identities and images.

Sailors, traders and other travellers worshipped the spirits of rivers as well as seas with prayers e.g. for a safe journey. These watery gods were just as scary and unknowable as the seas and inhabitants over whom they reigned, so Archaic Greek artists illustrated sea monsters - precursors of Aquaman and other mermen - with scary forms that combined human, animal, snake and/or fish parts. Heracles fought many such sea monsters. In his (now lost) 6th-century epic poem *Geryoneis*, stesichorus told us that Heracles asked Nereus-the old man of the sea and the father of the Nereids or sea nymphs- for directions to the home of Geryon. Nereus and his daughters, including Achilles' mother Thetis, had shape-changing powers.

Nereus' super power, to transform water into fire, might seem monstrous. If the pictures are to be believed, however, Heracles either hitched a ride on Nereus' scaly body, or grabbed a trip in the bowl of the sun (as detailed also by Pseudo-Apollodorus). In the latter case the route of direction would certainly be from East to West. We recognise the snaky-tailed older man decorating some vases as Nereus because the artist labelled him. Eventually this 'Old man of the sea' (*Halios Geron*) – as Homer calls him – appears just as an 'Old man' (*Geron*). I almost wonder if the poets saw a punning connection between *Geron* and Geryon, whom Heracles fought.

No sooner had the artists transformed Heracles' struggle with Nereus into a friendly encounter, then he battled another human-headed sea snake, namely Triton. By the third century BC *Tritones* comes in multiples: in ancient and Renaissance Rome they decorate tombs, temples, and fountains (cf. Bernini's 1643 Triton fountain in Rome). Much earlier, however, 6th-5th century Athenian pots show Heracles fighting a monster identified by the artists as 'Triton'. By the middle of the 6th century, Athenian artists shrink the monster's snaky body and bring the human heads of 'hero' and 'monster' close together. This encourages a comparison. Heracles-identifiable because he wears the skin of the Nemean lion-is literally level-headed; this suggests his intelligence that predicts his victory. Triton's larger head is bent down at an angle, from which position he fights to regain a foothold. As with the giants, the smaller 'hero' overpowers the larger 'monster'. Yet this is essentially a human or humanised battle, in which Heracles wins but doesn't kill.

Monsters test Heracles' strength and establish his popularity among mortals. Artists show Heracles' monstrous opponents as strong, even handsome, and increasingly human. This is especially the case with river and sea gods who are 'divine', like Heracles, yet shown increasingly in human form, again like Heracles. The myths tell us that – in his role as son of Zeus, the king of the Olympian gods – Heracles accomplished his labours to prove his divinity and join the gods on Mount Olympus. It is Heracles' humanity rather than his divinity, however, that brings his victory. Certainly Heracles' human appearance conditions us to see him as the protagonist and therefore the winner in his battles with monsters. Perhaps Heracles come out victorious simply because he is 'more human' than his snaky opponents.

Medusa,
by Evren Ozdemir

Dunstan Lowe

Dunstan Lowe is Senior Lecturer in Latin Literature at the University of Kent. He is the author of *Monsters and Monstrosity in Augustan Poetry* (University of Michigan Press, 2015). Another strand of his research is the reception of ancient myths in modern popular culture, especially video games, films and television. With Kim Shahabudin, he co-edited *Classics for All: Re-Working Antiquity in Mass Cultural Media* (Cambridge Scholars Publishing, 2009).

Classical monsters today

Although classical myth is a network of stories linked by geography, ancestry, and the activities of the Olympian gods, its monsters have a special hold on the collective imagination today. Most were originally one-off creatures of vast size and strength, occupying remote places in land or sea but hostile to all human visitors. Dangerous supernatural hybrids such as Gorgons and the Minotaur have become well known in Mediterranean and Western tradition, and are visually striking, making them easy to integrate in a range of modern media whether in their original narratives or not. They are distinctive to ancient Greece and Rome, and at the same time are easily compared with fantastical beings from other global cultures. From fine art and public monuments to movies and videogames, classical monsters have become familiar figures in the modern world's collective imagination-even though some have become very different from how they appeared in ancient sources. One example is Medusa, who was traditionally human-bodied and unarmed, but is often shown nowadays wielding a bow and with a snake's tail instead of legs. These details were only introduced by the sculpture that Ray Harryhausen designed and animated in 1981. It is important to realise that monsters could be portrayed quite flexibly, especially over time: Polyphemus the Cyclops was a popular theme in Roman art, but sometimes he had two or even three eyes instead of one. Perhaps the same process of change is at work when Centaurs gain armour, or when the bird-wings of Harpies become those of bats.

Unlike ancient texts and images, modern entertainment media often puts all the monsters of Greek myth in one place. A few were connected together by heroes who travelled far and wide – the Labours of Heracles, the quest of Jason and the Argonauts, and the voyages of Odysseus, Perseus, and Aeneas. In art, some complex projects assembled images from multiple stories: the Chest of Cypselus that was kept on display at Olympia for half a millennium bore images of the Hydra, Harpies, the three-bodied Geryon, and various Centaurs. Yet these belonged to different stories.

By contrast, twentieth- and twenty-first-century sources often collect classical monsters into a bestiary or roster of monster-types. Charles Finney's 1935 novella *The Circus of Dr Lao* (1935) assembled a Satyr, Sphinx, Chimera, and more at a travelling circus in rural America. This approach is typical of fantasy-themed games: in 1974, when the influential tabletop roleplaying game *Dungeons and Dragons* appeared, it presented a vast catalogue of supernatural creature-types. Although its main inspiration was sword-and-sorcery fiction, classical mythology conveniently supplied monstrous beings including Harpies, Minotaurs, and Medusas with distinctive appearances, habits, and abilities. Many videogames set in mythical Greece, such as the original *God of War* trilogy and more recently *Immortals: Fenyx Rising*, confront players with whole ecologies of monster enemies. Taken from separate stories, they have no consistent hierarchy. This is rather like what happened to Gothic horror, though classical monsters have stayed on the fringes of horror entertainment itself.

There is no equivalent to Dracula the 'prince of darkness' in classical antiquity-even the black Erinyes or Furies, who fly about their victims and torment them, are agents of justice who only punish the guilty. But modern re-imaginings of classical myth often look for an 'ultimate monster'. Some versions, like Disney's *Hercules*, turns the underworld's god Hades into an embodiment of evil, like the Christian Devil. The closest thing in classical antiquity is Typhoeus, who forms part of the origin-story of Zeus and the other Olympian gods, as told in the Theogony by the early poet Hesiod. The twelve Titans, including Kronos their ruler, were defeated by the twelve Olympians, led by Kronos' son Zeus: their mother Earth bore a grudge and later produced the Giants to attack Olympus, though they were hurled down and buried inside Earth herself, becoming fellow-prisoners of the Titans. In Hesiod's telling, Typhoeus was her last and greatest effort: a giant with a hundred serpent-heads, chaotically combining violent forces and discordant voices. Zeus defeats him in a duel, and the monster is absent from the rest of the myths to follow. The unclassical theme of the Titans and Typhoeus being unleashed again, to renew their assault against the Olympian gods, has gained popularity in the twenty-first century.

Modern storytelling about classical myth shows two strong urges that bring monsters into the limelight. First, there is a desire to reduce the gods to little more than superhumans, dependent on the support of mortals, who can be threatened and even destroyed. The first three *God of War* videogames are a good example of this, in which Kratos kills Ares and takes his place, and eventually revives the Titans for a new revolt against Olympus. Second, there is a desire for symmetrical conflict between forces of good and forces of evil (or at least, of order and disorder). This is well illustrated by Rick Riordan's Percy Jackson books, later expanded into a much larger franchise, in which the demigod schoolboy inhabits a modern-day world infused with Greek mythology. Monsters and heroes alike are continually reincarnated, hiding among humans and playing out ancient stories with sometimes humorous twists. The core narrative is once again that the Titans and their monstrous forces threaten the stability of a cosmos ruled by Zeus and the other gods.

A final change to the role of classical monsters in the twenty-first century is the trend of turning well-known narratives inside out, by moving the centre onto marginal or maligned figures, especially women. The cannibal beast-man killed by Theseus gets a sympathetic modern persona in Steven Sherrill's 2000 novel *The Minotaur Takes a Cigarette Break*. A sculpture by Luciano Garbati, in which Medusa holds the severed head of Perseus rather than the other way around, went viral in 2018 as an emblem of the #MeToo movement. Finally, Natalie Haynes's 2022 novel *Stone Blind* retells Medusa's story from the so-called monster's perspective, and even her severed head speaks.

Perhaps modern audiences now find it hard to allow the flawed Olympian gods their traditional privileges of human worship, cosmic power, and immortality. Or perhaps they are looking for fresh perspectives on the world of classical myth. Either way, ancient monsters seem to have almost as much appeal for modern-day audiences as for artists and authors in antiquity-who would be shocked by the stories we tell with them.

Phocomelia syndrome, from Hirst and Piersol, *Human Monstrosities* (1891-93)

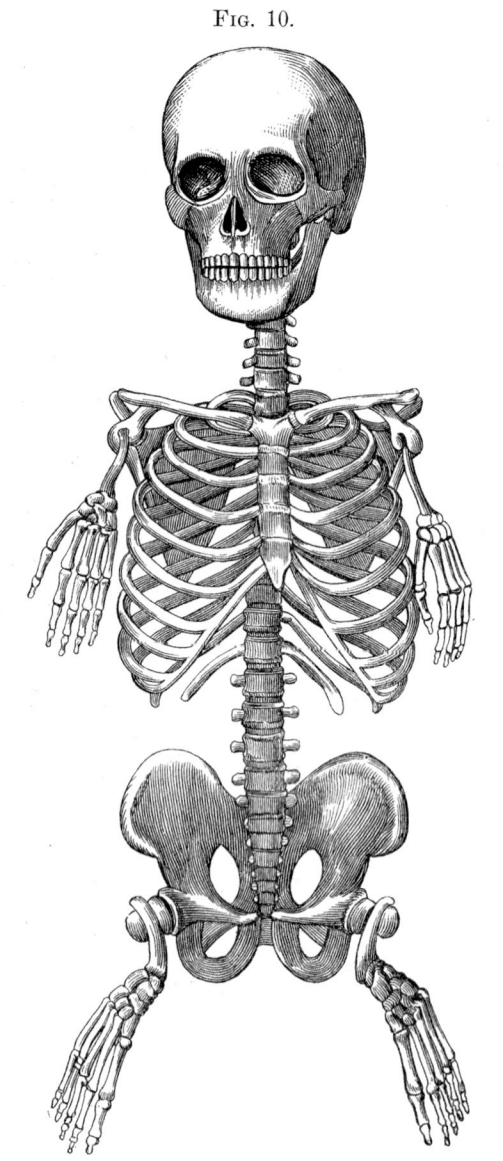

FIG. 10.

Skeleton of a phocomelus. (Musée Dupuytren.)

Andrew Mangham

Nature's experiments: Monsters in science and literature

Andrew Mangham is Professor of Victorian Literature and Medical Humanities at the University of Reading. He is the author of *We Are All Monsters: How Deviant Organisms Came to Define Us*. You can follow him on X @mangham.

We are used to thinking about monsters as outlandish, freakish, and *other* – as the strange and frightening inversions of our human values; yet, prior to the twentieth century, the biological sciences understood a *monster* to be an organism born with at least one permanent bodily defect or deformity. Such structural deformities could range from comparatively slight conditions such as a lack of pigment in the skin, to more serious singularities like the absence of a heart or brain. Historically, such defects had been linked to occult forces. Going back to antiquity, they had a long experience of being converted into warnings, often signifying the wrath of the gods, or a disaster about to happen. From the 1700s, however, monstrosity was also subjected to the pattern- and rule-finding powers of the physical sciences. In Jonathan Swift's *Gulliver's Travels* (1726), when the hero is among the giant Brobdingnagians, his tiny anatomy is classified as a 'sport of nature'. Although this term originated in the writings of Aristotle, and had originally implied that nature was vindictive and unkind – misshaping or deforming them for sport, the term also captures a newer understanding of bodies as made through a sort of universal creativeness. Nature isn't capriciously playing with our bodies, science suggested, it was trying new things. In the medical journal *The Lancet*, one surgeon wrote in 1847 that monstrosity is 'a sort of natural experiment'. Monsters came to represent the organic forces to which all life forms owe their major characteristics and strengths.

It is no coincidence that this redefinition of monstrosity occurred around the same time in history when notions on workings of organic life were revolutionised in Western science. This was the age of evolutionary theory, culminating in Charles Darwin's ground-breaking ideas of the mid-nineteenth century. According to the new science, organisms may shape-shift and morph into new types entirely. Was the atypical organism simply an example of a law of nature which is constantly trying new characteristics for species? Was the unusual characteristic the first step towards the evolution of one form into another? For example, it was common to wonder whether a person or animal born with extra digits was nature's way of trialling the usefulness of additional fingers and toes. According to the laws of evolution, any organism thriving with the extra digit would pass its singularity to the next generation, and a change to the species would gradually take place.

It was also around this time that the idea of the normal, or normality, was first defined. The earliest written evidence of the word 'normal' dates to 1777, suggesting perhaps that, against the new theories of evolution, where anything seemed possible, there was a need to pin down a sense of the usual – similar to how, in our own times, the growing prominence of trans people has encouraged some people to advocate a return to what they see as traditional definitions of male and female. However, it's much more likely that 'normal' was first defined in the age of evolutionary science, not because change and difference were contrary to the norm, but because they were a vital part of it. Singularities allowed scientists to see that, in nature, change and the atypical *are* the norm. In 1854, the amateur scientist George Henry Lewes insisted that 'monstrosities [are] *organic deviations*. They are not the products of hazard or caprice. They have their laws; these laws are the same as those which form all organisms; instead of escaping the general laws of organization, they only serve to prove the universality of those laws'. The monster, or, more accurately, 'monstrous development', was discovered, through the specialist mapping of natural laws, to reside at the very heart of the natural laws which shape us all.

In literature, this new idea was expanded into an exploration of what it is, fundamentally, that makes us human. While it is true that there has been an enduring fascination with monsters as freaks and gothic horrors, it is also true that alongside these colourful representations has been a determination to make the same figures ask important questions about the human condition. In Mary Shelley's *Frankenstein* (1818), for example, the artificial man at the heart of the classic novel is called 'monster' a total of sixteen times – mainly by other characters but also, interestingly, by the creature himself. Contrary to how he was represented in Hollywood films, the artificial man of Shelley's novel is articulate, intelligent, and introspective. 'Was I then a monster, a blot upon the earth, from which all men fled, and whom all men disowned?' he asks. He reports the first time he sees his reflection: 'I started back, unable to believe that it was indeed I who was reflected in the mirror'. He comes to realise, 'I was in reality the monster that I am'. *Frankenstein*'s famous monster recognises his selfhood and his physical uniqueness all in the same moment. The powerful words 'monster that I am' acknowledge both a distinctiveness ('monster') and a self ('I am'). It is only when he comes into contact with other humans who show intolerance of his differences that he learns to know his monstrosity as something that is unnatural and wrong. It is also in response to the same intolerance that the creature turns violent, transforming his difference from a fascinating study of what it is that makes us human, into gothic horror. But what if the creature had discovered a more tolerant world, alert to the fact that difference is what allows us to develop and evolve? Like the science of the time, Shelley's novel invites us to ask important questions about the atypical as central to who we are, what we are capable of, and the prices we pay for narrow-mindedness.

Catalogue
Eleanor Crook

1. *The Great God Pan*
Oil on canvas
13 x 13

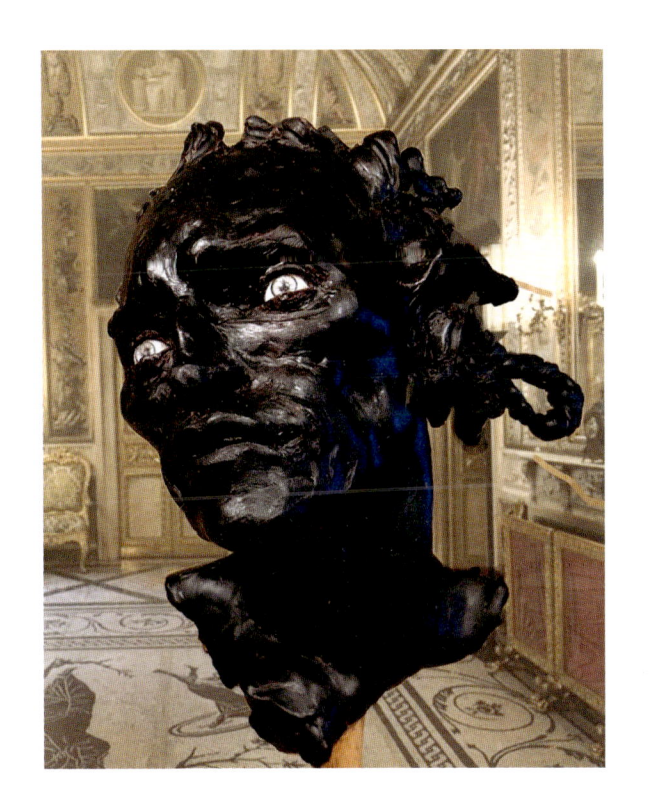

2. *Fates*
Bronze
Each 20 x 13 x 13

3. *Sybil's Head*
Bronze
32 x 24 x 24

4. *Eustache 'Jerk' Dupree, the Icarus Man of Pontchartoula*
Wax and mixed media
26 x 45 x 20

5. *Marsyas*
Bronze
71 x 31 x 44 S

6. *Rex Pulmonum (King of the Lungs)*
Patinated bronze
45 x 25 x 27

4. *Charon Sank*
AI Print

5. *Fossilised Minotaur*
AI Print

6. *Queen of Midas*
AI Print

7. *The Golden Bough*
AI Print

8. *Nietzsche-Cow/Dionysus*
Bronze
70 x 15 x 27

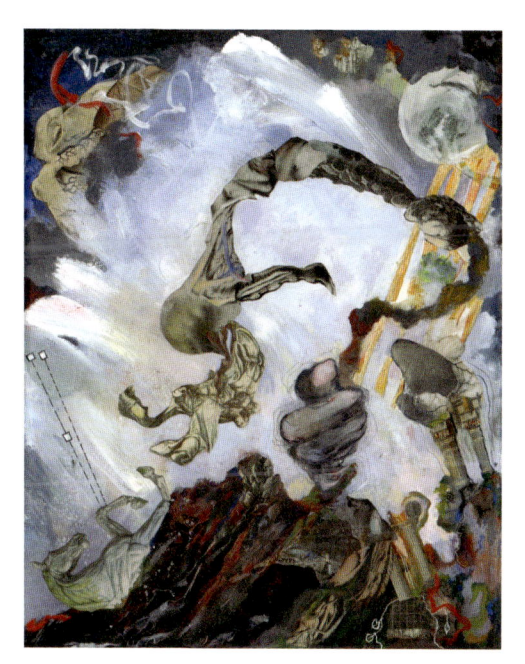

9. Triptych *(Orpheus Lives, Sisyphus Quits, Icarus Flies)*
Mixed media
Each 50 x 41

10. *Centaur*
High-patinated Bronze
71 x 59 x 43

11. *Underworld Series*
Mixed media
Each 40 x 40

Paul Reid

12. *Cyclops*
Oil on canvas
122 x 137

13. *Gigantomachy study*
Charcoal and ink on board
62 x 79

14. *Dionysus with Lion*
Acrylics on board
62 x 79

15. *Diana*
Oil on canvas
22.25 x 24

16. *Odysseus on the Island of Circe*
Oil on canvas
106.5 x 130.5

17. *Apollo and Pan*
Oil on canvas
122 x 137

18. *Hermes and Argos*
Oil on canvas
30 x 50

19. Minotaur
Oil on canvas
100 x 75

20. *Pan*
Oil on canvas
88 x 98

21. *Pan, Hermes & Typhon*
Ink/acrylic on board
106.5 x 130.5

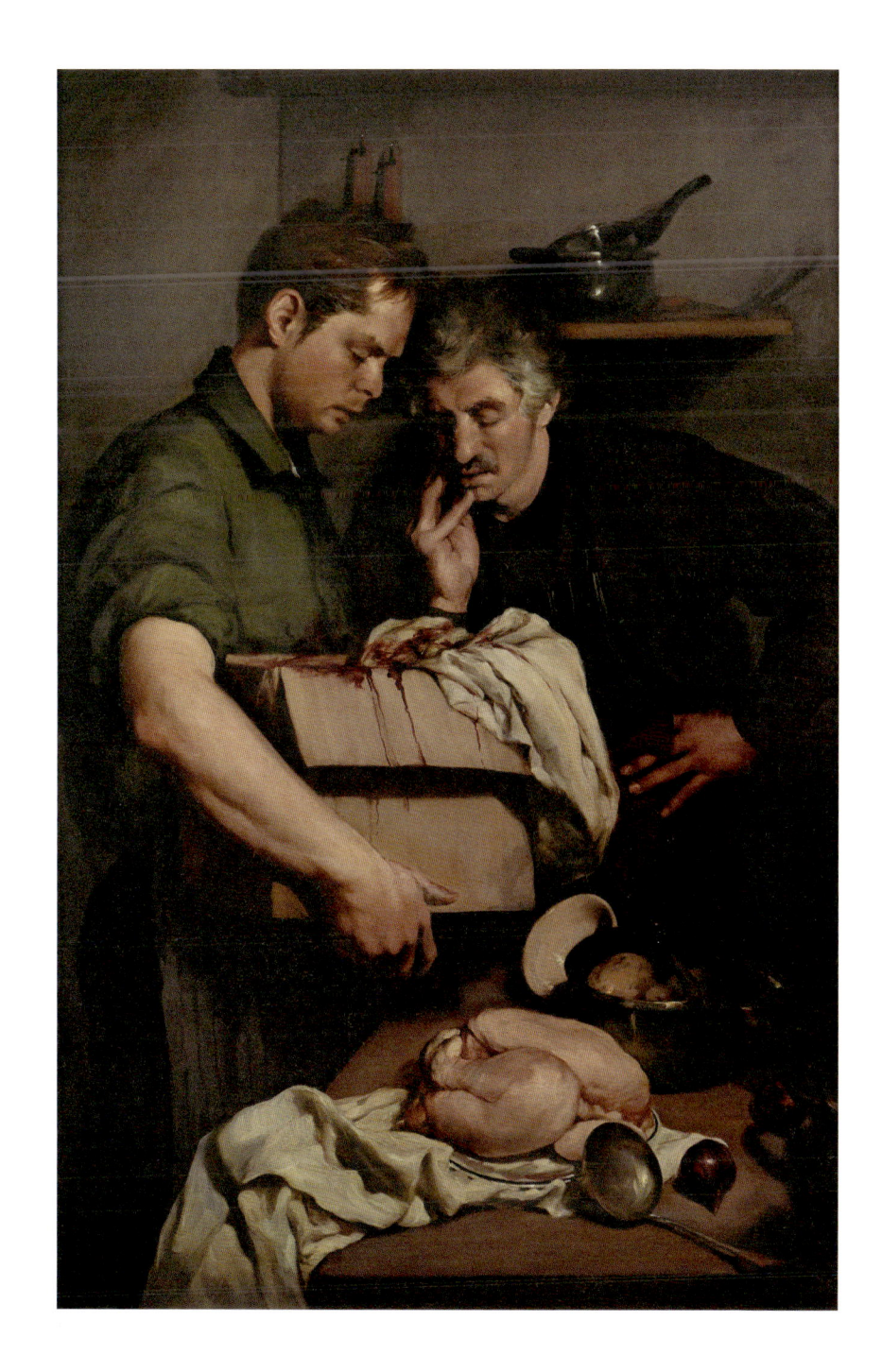

22. *Lycaon's Cooks*
Oil on canvas
152.4 x 91.4

23. *Theseus and the Minotaur*
Oil on canvas
122 x 137

24. *Actaeon*
Oil on canvas
83.5 x 98

25. *Portrait of Pan*
Printed on 310gm Hahnemuhle
German etching paper
60 x 39.5

26. *Study for Pan*
Ink on paper
49 x 50

27. *Minotaurs*
Acrylic on board
45 x 60

Michael Ayrton

28. *Minotaur Revealed*
Etching on paper
55 x 42

29. *Minotaur as Calf*
Etching on paper
55 x 42

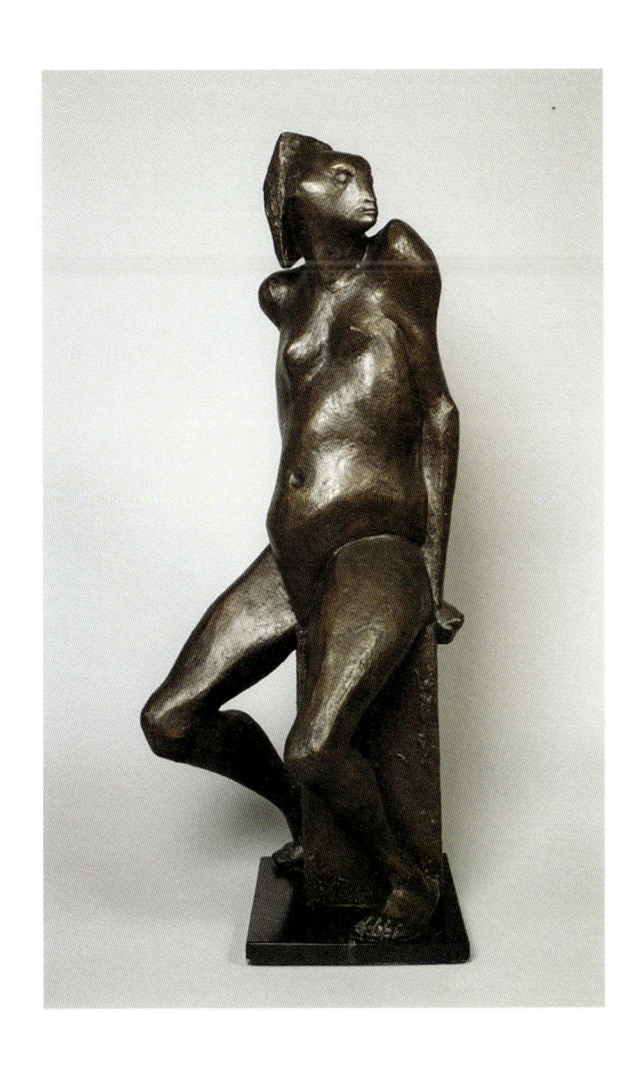

30. *Demeter Pregnant*
Bronze
79 x 30 x 30

31. *Turning Maze Runner*
Charcoal on laid paper
95 x 72.5

32. *Minotaur Waking*
Bronze
30 x 30 x 30

Minnie Jane Hardman

33. *Venus de Milo*
Charcoal on laid paper
60.6 x 46.8

34. *Study of Wrestlers*
Charcoal and graphite on wove paper
75.5 x 50.5

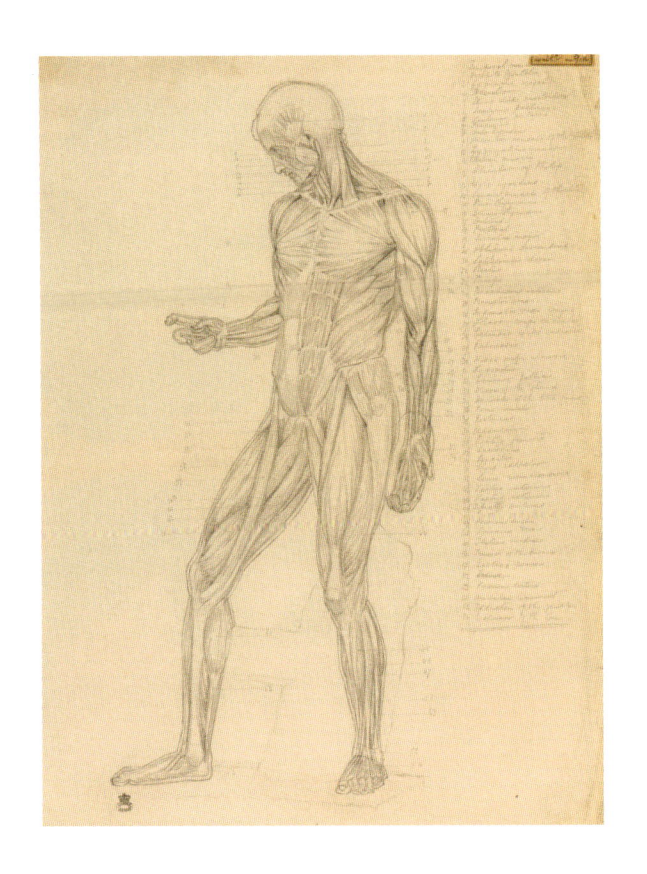

35. *Discophoros écorché*
Ink on wove paper
78 x 55.9

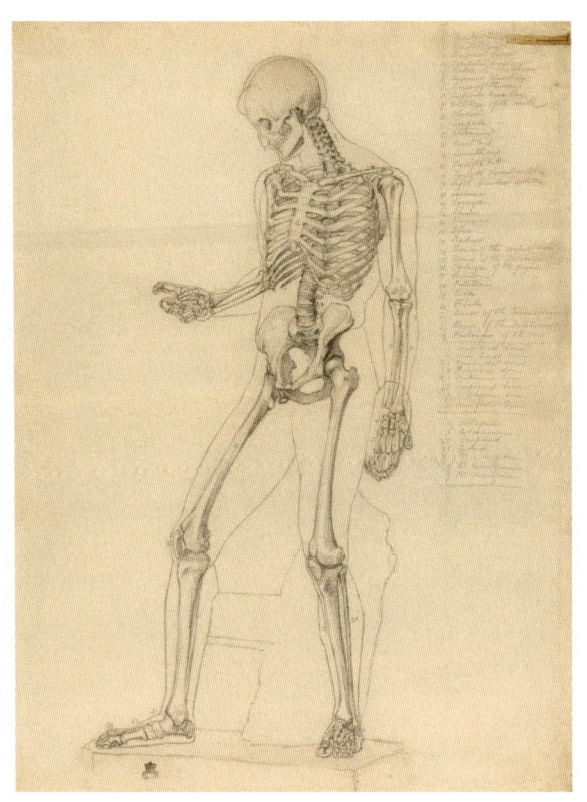

36. *Discophoros skeleton*
Ink on wove paper
78 x 55.9

37. *Discophoros*
Graphite on wove paper
73.8 x 45.1

38. *Study of Hercules*
Graphite on wove paper
73.7 x 54.5